The Game of Life

Edu Petriati

Published by Edu Petriati, 2024.

While every precaution has been taken in the preparation of this book, the publisher assumes no responsibility for errors or omissions, or for damages resulting from the use of the information contained herein.

THE GAME OF LIFE

First edition. May 12, 2024.

ISBN: 979-8224221073

Written by Edu Petriati.

This book is a translation from the Spanish book El Juego de la Vida, from the same author. Both versions were released on the same day.
Cover Design by Luisina De Sagastizábal
Instagram @luisinadesa

INTRODUCTION

Two decades ago, a book changed my life, offering me answers to deep questions I had carried with me from my upbringing in a Catholic home and school. Thomas Campbell's "My Big Toe," which means My Big Theory of Everything, became a beacon for me in a sea of uncertainty. This trilogy, later compiled into a single volume, details the teachings Campbell acquired through his experience with Bob Monroe in the early days of the Monroe Institute.

The book thoroughly breaks down how our reality, the universe, consciousness, and evolution work. In the end, it sheds light on the fundamental reason for our existence and our purpose in this vast cosmos.

At the same time, my personal interest in astrology has been a constant throughout my life. I began to delve into its complexities in search of answers about who we are, where we come from, and where we are headed. Over time and through personal experiences, I came to understand that astrology is not simply a set of beliefs, but a powerful tool for self-exploration and understanding the world around us.

Astrology, from the interpretation of a natal chart to the analysis of planetary transits, offers a map of our existence. Although it does not determine our destiny, it provides us with valuable explanations about our tendencies, our motivations and the cycles that influence our lives.

In this book, we will explore the soul's journey to Earth and how, once incarnated, our lives become intertwined with the movements of the planets. Those familiar with astrology will be able to identify patterns in our protagonist's natal chart and anticipate significant events in her life. For those less versed in astrology, this information will be a guide to better understand how the stars influence our lives and decisions.

Ultimately, this writer's goal is to invite reflection on the cyclical nature of life and the eternal transformation of being. It is a reminder that, although cycles have a beginning and an end, life continues in an infinite spiral of experiences and learning.

THE JOURNEY TO EARTH

The protagonist of this adventure is Celeste, who is in the process of defining her new arrival on earth. We could define her as an old soul since she has gone through several incarnations and countless experiences and tests until reaching this present, where something new is about to be experienced.

She, beyond the fact that in this present game she is known as Celeste, has already gone through different characters before, in different circumstances, times and places. She now finds herself in the place where the selection of conditions is carried out to go to earth as a new participant.

Each one who returns to an experience on earth will have to specify under what conditions it will go, even though they are selections of beginning, not development. Free will exists and it is exercised by all participants in the game, which means that the possibilities and alternatives of what will happen are infinite.

Celeste at this moment is conscious energy and by her decision she returns to incarnate in the game of life, and she is deciding what her part will be.

She has to choose her parents, the place where she is born, and then she waits for the conditions to be given to the 'parents' she chose for conception to occur, and to be able to descend to the plane of the earth.

At this moment Celeste is aware of all her previous participations and the result of each of them. Now she chooses something different to experience and adds to her extensive history and experiences.

Although Celeste's essence is immortal and has its hierarchical position within a certain universal structure, she knows that when she arrives on earth, she will not remember any of that and even more so, she will be assigned certain characteristics that are not her own but come from her parents' family trees. That is to say, the tree of these two families each has its own story and must be continued. Celeste has no control over that, but those will be conditions that she must carry out to fulfill her objective, which 'she' herself agreed with what she intends to achieve.

After having filled out all the information regarding her character, that information is managed by artificial intelligence (AI) which has the information of all the participants on earth at this time, and will give her the OK to go, when the parents' conditions are given.

Celeste fills out the required information as follows:

Father: free-spirited, calm, affable

Mother: strong character, with a lot of drive and ambition. This is because she wants to live the experience of a domineering and entrepreneurial mother, something she did not have in her previous experiences.

Location: city with tradition but not a megapolis. With this she wants to experience living in a city that, although it has all the characteristics of an important city, also has less hustle and bustle.

Nationality or other specific characteristics are not chosen, but elements are sought that lead them to overcome aspects that they previously did not resolve satisfactorily and to be able to share their previously acquired knowledge and add to the common good.

All this information is processed by AI and searched among all possible actors that meet the requested conditions.

The AI searches among the millions of possible candidates for parents who are included within the conditions requested and for family trees that Celeste can face according to her previously acquired capacity, and thereby develop new skills that were not completely overcome in past lives.

The AI would never assign something that the soul cannot fulfill, this would make no sense on an individual or collective level. Whether each person can overcome the situations they face will depend on the actions that each person takes, and depending on that, things will have their result. The result is already part of what each participant does and other circumstances that intervene when it happens. Let us remember that the memory is erased upon arrival, so the tests not previously passed will have the possibility of being completed in the following experiences.

Celeste is notified to prepare because for a certain date on earth (which is different from the universal one) she will go through the process of transmutation from the current state to the new life that will be created.

This is known because the system warns that the conditions of the selected parents are in place for conception.

Celeste gets ready, her 'friends' bid her farewell and tell her that they will be eagerly waiting for her to return so she can tell everything that happened during this new experience.

Celeste enters the specialized place for the distribution of souls that incarnate. She enters a very spacious and bright place, where there are many bed-type chairs with an integrated control panel. They guide Celeste into one, and she lies back very comfortably and waits for the activation.

In a moment it is like a bubble of light appears on the chair where she is lying and a movement begins, a great acceleration forward and she enters a tunnel of light, she sees the galaxies, the planets, the solar system, the earth and suddenly, nothing.

She doesn't remember anything, her mind is blank... Silence, darkness, nothingness...

...Celeste, who has not yet been born, but is in a state of gestation in the mother, has already been assigned the genetic load of her parents and her ancestors distributed in different proportions in her DNA, which was determined at the time of gestation.

During her pregnancy she goes through all the same moods as the mother. From a certain moment onwards, she listens to the music that the mother listens to, feels the taste of what the mother eats, feels her joys and sadness, and creates a bond with the mother which will unite them for the entire duration of this experience.

Celeste forgot where she came from, she was in the water, she didn't know where, but it gave her protection and warmth, she could even move! She felt that she shared everything with someone who still did not know that she was her mother, that kept her company, she did not feel alone.

Time passes and the sensations increase, and she feels tight where she is, she used to be comfortable before, until at a certain moment something happens.

There is a crisis, movements, the water in which she was immersed disappears, the squeezing begins, she does not know what is happening.

A moment later she is in another place, away from her mother...

What is this? What happened here? All confusion, all foreign, all chaos.

In that moment of chaos and confusion, Celeste is born. The nurse looks at the clock on the wall of the delivery room and writes 12:40 AM on the chart.

THE BEGINNINGS OF CELESTE

The place, date, and time where the person is born, is the basis of the natal chart, which has a parallel to the information of the DNA is some aspects.

The natal chart imprints the planet's energy and characteristics of that moment into the newborn and starts the clock marking the energy cycles that will follow the person throughout life. It's all part of a comprehensive system where the meticulous work of the AI selected the best path to reach this moment, based on the information entered by Celeste and all the background information that already existed.

Everything has the objective of fulfilling a purpose.

The Sun was in the sign of Virgo, which becomes her zodiacal sign, with an ascendant in the sign of Gemini. These signs provide certain characteristics and attributes that we will see how they will manifest themselves as we go through her life.

The parents, the grandparents, the uncles, the whole family happy and excited about the newcomer. Everyone is going to give their welcome, they give their opinion to who she resembles, it is a moment where love and good energy abounds which fills Celeste, even though she is not aware of everything that happens.

Celeste doesn't understand anything, she only knows that when she is hungry and when she feels uncomfortable in her diaper she has to cry. It seems that that interaction works well, because when she cries, she has a response to crying.

It is the first communication that this being of light, who has already gone through this countless times, but she does not remember it.

That's getting to the game of life. It is not the entrance through the front door with all the previous recognitions with fanfare, but to the basics of human existence. Get fed, get cleaned and get nurtured.

From that moment on, Celeste begins to go through her life's cycles. She enters a game that has the same rules and objectives as elsewhere, but here they manifest themselves differently. Feelings are something very particular to human beings and this plane. Although the entire universe works with mathematical rules, when feelings come into play, two plus two can equal five! Boolean algebra sometimes doesn't work as expected, especially among human relationships. But this is not necessarily bad, everything has an explanation.

Celeste's natal chart has the following characteristics, Jupiter and Venus in the 1st house, Uranus in the 2nd house, Pluto and Mars in the 3rd house, the Moon, the Sun and Mercury in the 4th house, Saturn in the 10th house and Neptune in the 11th house.

According to her natal chart, we can define the following general characteristics for Celeste:

The Sun in Virgo gives her the characteristic of being meticulous, orderly, and mental, in addition by being a woman, this sign gives her additional charm. Her Gemini ascendant makes her attractive, witty, and able to connect with others.

Jupiter in the first house gives her the characteristics of being spontaneous and charismatic, with a good capacity to fascinate others. Her Venus, which is also in her first house, will cause Celeste to value her personal aesthetics throughout her life, adding this to her natural charm and making her appear visually attractive.

Uranus in the Second House predicts economic ups and downs during her life. She will look for a way to not be tied to her income with a need for freedom and liberation in that aspect, which will often lead to unexpected changes and disruptions on the economic level.

Deep thoughts and a powerful mind, but since Pluto and Mars are in the house of communication, she can become very passionate, intense, direct, crude, and even tactless.

Contact with others could be distant during childhood and we will see how she handles it when she is an adult.

The Sun, Moon, and Mercury in the fourth house of the home have a very profound influence on emotional security and family dynamics. Her identity is closely tied to her family background and the experiences she has growing up. Her roots are very important to Celeste, they give her a sense of belonging. The Moon gives her deep intuition and emotional intelligence. Mercury predicts a home full of books, where adult topics can be discussed with her when growing up, where education is very important.

Since Saturn is in her tenth house, it generates great ambitions and also high standards in what her intellectual development and profession will be. She will not shy away from working hard to achieve her goals. She will take on responsibilities without thinking.

Finally, Neptune in the eleventh house gives her creativity and imagination. She will be comfortable with spiritual and metaphysical topics, and she will have a good understanding of the collective unconscious.

These are the conditions with which Celeste arrives on earth's plane. They are characteristics that she does not yet understand and that she will begin to show as she grows. Certain characteristics can be seen from a young age, others will be seen when the cycles of her life begin to manifest, mainly at 7, 14 and 28 years old and then between 40 and 43. This last cycle which is the opposition of Uranus, It is the first part of life, from which the person can evaluate what are the results obtained from the combination of the natal characteristics, the astrological cycles and the important decisions that were made using free will.

The opposition of Uranus provides the opportunity to analyze what happened during the first half of life, to make changes on areas that did not went well, in order to improve one's life for the second part.

That's how Celeste's life begins, which is no different to any other participant in the game of life on earth.

CELESTE'S CHILDHOOD

Celeste grows and increases her participation within an environment of family and acquaintances, whom she begins to recognize and starts establishing a connection with. With some she felt more affinity, with others less, although everyone treated her very well. She liked to be in the company of people.

It is a stage in Celeste's life where things are very simple. The days go by without any major surprises, and she begins to recognize flavors, foods, crawl, stand up, take the first steps...

So, her life goes by with increases in activities and participation, without any major surprises that we can mention for a girl who already is 10 years old.

Suddenly, the first major crisis in Celeste's life.

A tremendous problem between the parents leads to their separation and Celeste moving with her mother to her maternal grandparent's house. It is a critical period, not only for an adult, but also for someone who is growing.

We could mention this as the first crisis of Uranus in the second house, that even though she currently has no income, family finances have an effect on her.

The cause of her parents' separation is due to financial problems on the part of the father, where having invested in businesses that did not give the expected results affected the stability of the family. Something similar had already happened before, and Celeste's mother was the one who had to come to the rescue of the situation. On this second occasion, there was no settlement and her parents ended up separating.

Coincidentally, in Celeste's natal chart, transiting Pluto entered her fourth house, the house related to home. This is not only producing a crisis in Celeste's life, but also anticipates a very unstable time for the coming years, since Pluto will conjunct her Moon, the Sun and Mercury during its transit through the fourth house.

While it is a time of crisis, it is also a time of seeing the family in action. From both sides of Celeste's grandparents and uncles are of great help and support during this period.

At this point it is valid to clarify something that is fundamental for understanding 'the game of life'. Although Celeste set conditions for her arrival and these were met as she expressed, when she arrives at earth level, she finds that one of the conditions of the game is free will.

She and all the participants who are in the game knew that, so the decisions made by each of the known or external characters, are their own responsibility, and that means that it is uncertain how the game will develop. We know how it begins, but we don't know how it evolves or how it ends. That's what's exciting and enigmatic about this game.

Any video game is designed just like the game of life is, but with the big difference that the characters involved are 'limited' in their actions, decisions, and movements. The video game has its limits that may be given by processing speed, programming complexity, costs and so on, but in the Game of Life this does not happen.

Astrology somehow gives us a hint with the planet's cycles. In the game of life cycles are repeated, it is not something linear although we have this perception. In the game we go through the same cycle in some cases every month, in others once in a lifetime, but those that are repeated, since each planet has a different translation, we never encounter exactly the same conditions. That is why it is defined that the trend of the cycle is the same, but the effect varies.

Considering these conditions nobody can predict the future. It is like the weather forecast, it is said that there is a possibility of rain in percentages, whether this happens will depend on other factors which could change the expected trend.

In the information that Celeste entered regarding what she requested to return to earth, she defined a certain characteristic of her parents and the place, but she could not define that the parents should not separate because that would violate the free will of other participants. and that cannot be done.

He who violates that rule of the game of life on earth will at some point have to face the consequences. This at higher levels does not even appear as an option, beyond the fact that someone with a higher degree of consciousness would not do it even if it was allowed.

It should also be mentioned that there are guides, which cannot be seen, but are there to help in the game. These guides are available 24 hours a day, but to understand this, requires a certain openness to other dimensions that is often not achieved for different reasons. Similar to astrology, many times the scope or purpose is misled or not understood. These guides will try to communicate in different ways, but without intervening directly, we could call them 'advisors'.

In essence, what was mentioned above are the basic rules and conditions of the game.

Now let's see how our protagonist continues, this is just the beginning...

It is the period where Celeste begins her studies. She likes school. She is interested in what they teach her. She is entertained, it opens her imagination.

Celeste may have glimpses of what she was before arriving at earth, she has dreams, or imagines of different things, she is attracted to the sky, the stars. At night she contemplates the sky as if searching for something, it attracts her. She put so much attention to the sky that even she recognizes some satellites that orbit the earth and knows time and direction when they pass. What's out there attracts her, it activates her search for knowledge, it is instinctive, she doesn't know why, but she feels a connection to something she doesn't see.

She lives with her grandparents and her mother and has a quiet life. She makes friends where she lives, and they play for hours and hours creating things, inventing games, watching movies. Beyond her social life, which is participatory, she spends hours playing alone, or reading. She doesn't mind being alone, she feels comfortable with herself.

Beyond all the problems that have occurred, it is like she has everything she needs.

Her mother works in a company that sells highly complex medical devices. She has a managerial position which demands a lot of time. She has led a successful career in the company and may have been one of the reasons for her divorce. Celeste's father, who is a merchant and has his own business, is more relaxed, less ambitious and conformist.

They both feel a deep love for Celeste and even though they no longer live together, she enjoys every moment she is with each of them.

Celeste's father takes her for walks, to the movies, to amusement parks, it is entertaining, and she enjoys the time with him.

Celeste's mother, after her intense days of work, tries to relax and rest during her free time. The education of her daughter is important to her, and it is common for her to share with Celeste articles, books or topics that help stimulate Celeste's curiosity and learning. She would like her daughter to be successful in her life, so that she can have professional development like she achieved. These are times of change at a social level.

Celeste's maternal grandfather worked for an aviation company, so he had free tickets as long as there was room on the flights. Celeste loved the trips she took with her grandparents to different states to visit relatives and friends of hers. It was usually the big summer adventure during school holidays. Although it was vacation and recreation, sharing the house with others, where there were also half cousins and others her age, was something new. New entertainment, new adventures, new experiences.

On vacation the daily routine changed completely, and it was much more active than during school time.

She had weekend getaways with his mother, where they usually went to the beach. Both Celeste and her mother loved the sea and had access to it within a few hours' drive. Since she was little, Celeste enjoyed playing with the sand, entering, and leaving the water. She felt free and connected to the water, which although she did not think about it, was under the environment that her gestation took place. Her Sun and Moon in Virgo asked her to be in contact with water, it balanced her energies.

Celeste liked school vacation periods a lot, it allowed her to change her routine, it opens the possibility to see and discover other things.

This is how she spends her elementary studies where she is very applied and recognized for her ability and performance. She appears on the honor roll year after year.

Her mother or grandparents never had to worry about doing homework and studying. Celeste was very responsible in that regard.

The time of high school arrives, where friends of the opposite sex are already beginning to be interested. She does not have a hectic social life, but she had already formed a group of friends, some from school, others childhood friends and friends of friends.

To understand why a person acts in a certain way or understand what is going on in his or her mind, an astrological analysis provides some answers by describing the natal characteristics according to the natal chart.

Let's quickly see the profile that Celeste has according to her natal chart.

She may be perceived by others as someone who is ambitious and caring, with a magnetic personality and a strong sense of emotional intelligence.

Her ambitious nature, indicated by Saturn in the 10th house and Jupiter in the 1st house, would make her appear motivated, goal-oriented and determined. Others may see her as someone capable, responsible, and trustworthy, with a clear vision for her future and the discipline for her to work hard to achieve her goals.

At the same time, her protective qualities, highlighted by the Moon, Sun and Mercury in the fourth house, would make her appear warm, affectionate, and empathetic. She can be perceived as someone deeply connected to her family and roots, with a strong sense of loyalty and dedication towards her loved ones. Others may look to her for comfort, support, and guidance, knowing that she is always there to listen or help.

Her magnetic personality, indicated by Venus in the 1st house, would make her naturally attractive and charismatic. Others may be attracted to her warmth, charm and grace and find her company enjoyable and uplifting. She may have a way of making people feel valued and appreciated, fostering strong connections and lasting relationships wherever she goes.

Overall, she would probably be perceived as someone who embodies a unique combination of ambition, caring, and charisma. Her ability to balance her drive toward success with her compassion for others would make her stand out in any social or professional setting, earning the respect, admiration, and affection of those around her.

This is a very quick astrological analysis of Celeste at this time of her life, and how other people perceive her.

From this moment on, is when the exercise of her free will begins to take precedence and is when Celeste will begin to receive the results of her actions.

It is a period that all human beings go through, and each one will be able to remember how it acted or reacted to situations and what consequences, if any, they had over time.

THE UNIVERSITY

Celeste finishes her higher education and is ready to go to university. During the various aptitude tests she had, added to the information that her mother shared over the years, and considering the scientific advances of the moment, it was no surprise to find that her profile gave her a chance for technical careers, beyond what she already knew. Also, Uranus in the second house could hint income related to technology.

She received an invitation from a couple of universities to which she had applied and after talking with her mother she decided to go to the one located in another state.

Although Celeste was always surrounded by family and that fulfilled her, she also had the need to spread her wings and leave the nest. This created mixed emotions in her.

She had decided to go to another state, where she would not have the family protection around like she had. She knew she was going to be alone, even though communication with family and friends could be frequent. She also knew that if she needed it, she was just a call away for them to come to her aid.

These emotions that Celeste felt had an explanation from an astrological point of view; She was already beginning to feel the effects of the first square of Uranus, and this would be followed by the second square of Saturn.

The first square of Uranus affects her economy. She is having to deal with expenses now, something that she did not have to worry about before. There are expenses for the apartment, mobility, and maintenance for which she will use the money that was in the savings account her mother years ago opened for her studies, in addition to a scholarship that the university offered her.

It is a period of increased responsibility, which will climax when Saturn has its return. But don't let get ahead of ourselves.

There were several branches in the area of technology that interested her, but since the first 2 years were common to all, she decided to start and later define the major to graduate.

After parties and goodbyes, tears and jokes, Celeste set out in her new direction. This is a very important moment in any person's life, and when free will was mentioned, this is a good example of how a person's life can have a transcendental turn according to the decisions made.

Once located in a small apartment near the university, Celeste settles in, preparing her new home with the warmth and shelter under which she grew up, and it is something that she values and is very important to her. She likes plants, so it is one of the first things she bought to decorate and set the mood for the apartment, which already came furnished and with the basic things for two people.

Since she has a few days left before classes start, she walks around the neighborhood to familiarize herself with the surrounding businesses and see the cafes and food places available.

The long-awaited day arrives, and classes begin.

Celeste feels a combination of excitement and nervousness as she faces the new environment that she only knew from different references. She is excited to begin this new stage of her life, but also thinking about her adaptation to a new place, meeting new classmates and learning to navigate the campus, which really surprises her because of the excellent facilities it has.

By the end of the first week, it felt like she had been there for a long time. She begins to organize her routine, her schedule, and the books she needed for each class.

She has long conversations with her mother, telling in detail everything that happened. Her mother gives her advice relating to the experiences she went through when she was in the same situation as her.

Celeste's mother feels fulfilled, proud of her daughter who took that leap. She felt like she had achieved a goal in her life and that everything she had worked to support Celeste's education was paying off.

One day follows another, Celeste begins to meet classmates, they get together for meals, they go out for drinks, little by little she makes new friends.

This is how the first semesters go by where she advances in different subjects without any problem. She attends meetings, college football games, little by little she begins to enjoy her new life.

She maintained fluid communication with her grandparents, her mother, her father, and the friends she had left behind. Some of them remained in the city, others went to other colleges.

She only returned home for spring break vacation or yearend holidays which she enjoyed, but now from a different perspective. Little by little she detached herself from her past, which remained in memories and anecdotes, and integrating more into this new part of her life.

By the second year she had already defined her career, which was Computer Science, with an application to robotics. She was interested in intelligent prostheses. She was attracted to new technologies and saw the humanitarian side in the application of robotics to help people regain mobility and handling so they could function fully again.

Apart from reading class books, doing her practical work and projects, with the curious mind she had, she constantly looked for other topics not related to school, and she came across astrology. A while ago she had drawn her attention to some things she had read, but since at that time there were other topics that caught her attention more, she left it aside. At this moment she was interested in knowing a little more and she was marking articles and blogs to delve deeper into the topic.

She made her natal chart online and read about what each planet represented in her chart. Several things she found interesting piqued her curiosity even more. How can my natal chart say this about me? Not because it was bad, but because there was a lot of similarity with how she was.

In conversations with classmates, she did not find much echo from them about what she had discovered in astrology. Conversation usually derived in jokes about the zodiacal sign of each one of those present, and generally the negative aspect of each one's sign to the laughter of the group.

ALEX

In the heart of a bustling metropolis lived a boy named Alex. He grew up in a modest apartment with his loving parents who worked tirelessly to support the family. Despite the challenges of city life, Alex found solace and joy in two things: sports and studies.

From a young age, Alex showed a natural talent for athletics. Whether it was soccer games in the park or basketball games on the neighborhood court, he thrived in the competitive spirit of sports. However, in addition to his passion for physical activity, Alex possessed an insatiable curiosity to learn. He immersed himself in books, absorbing knowledge like a sponge.

While navigating the challenges of adolescence and adulthood, Alex remained dedicated to his dual goals. Excelling in both academics and sports, he found himself on a promising path toward a career in the medical field. Driven by the desire to make a difference in the world and help others, everything related to care and attention to the sick completely met his objectives.

The effort he had put into sports paid off, as he was offered a scholarship from a university if he became part of the basketball team. Alex came from a middle-class home and the cost of college was more than they could afford. They had evaluated the possibility of taking out a loan for the degree and the scholarship was like a gift from heaven for Alex and his parents.

It was during his college years when Alex's life took an unexpected turn. In the always busy hallways of the university, he crossed paths with a girl who would change everything. Her name was Celeste, and from the moment Alex saw her, he was captivated by her intelligence, her beauty, and her excellent sense of humor.

Celeste was unlike anyone Alex had ever met before. She challenged him intellectually, engaging him in stimulating conversations that sparked his imagination. Her laugh was music to his ears, brightening even the darkest days. With every moment he spent in her presence, Alex fell more and more in love with her.

Their relationship blossomed in the context of their demanding studies and busy lives. They supported each other through the long hours of studying and the pressures of exams, finding comfort and strength in each other's arms. Together, they celebrated victories and overcame challenges, and their bond grew stronger with each passing day.

As graduation approached and their future loomed on the horizon, Alex and Celeste knew their love was something special. With the world at their feet and a lifetime of adventures ahead of them, they embarked on the next chapter of their journey together, hand in hand, ready to face any challenge that came their way.

For Alex, the boy who had grown up in the city with the dream of making a difference had found his greatest adventure of all in the love of a girl who had stolen his heart. And together they knew that their love would be the greatest adventure of all.

Alex had his dorm at the university, and it wasn't far from Celeste's apartment. That made it possible to spend moments together.

Through university, Celeste had obtained an internship at a company that was in the same city, and it did not take long for the company to notice the ability and knowledge that Celeste had, so they offered her a permanent position managing the priority that her target was graduating.

Alex also did some part-time jobs always related to the medical part, so they were both well occupied between university and jobs.

The last semester before graduation was very active for both. Between college and the jobs, they had, the days flew by, until graduation day arrived.

Celeste's mother, father, and grandmother are going to graduation as are Alex's parents. Although everyone was aware of the relationship between Celeste and Alex, each one kept their celebration separate.

Another chapter in Celeste's life is completed and a new one begins.

A NEW ROAD

There were conversations between Celeste and her mother regarding her future and the topic of work was discussed. Celeste listened to her mother's advice since she respected her knowledge and wisdom. Celeste felt good in the company she worked for, she had a job in which she could apply part of what she learned at the university, but more than anything, she could learn much more about things that she had only heard about during her studies. The work was like a postgraduate degree, she continually learned something new, and she liked that a lot.

Her mother told her, it is not common for someone to stay working for lifetime in their first job. Always keep an open mind as the world is more than that, there can always be other opportunities for something better. While Celeste understood the message, this was the time to stay where she was and not look for another job. That meant that she would stay living where she was. It was a two-hour plane ride to her natal place. She could go on long weekends or during vacation.

And that's how Celeste stayed in her new home, already thinking about what her next steps would be like, but she would talk about that with Alex to see if they would decide something together.

Alex had finished his scholarship, so he returned to his parents' house for a few days to see what possibilities he had.

Celeste returns to her grandparents' house to celebrate her 24th birthday. She can't wait to share this moment with her family and friends. Although this is a quick trip due to her work responsibilities, her excitement at reuniting with her family and her friends fills her with joy. The house is decorated with balloons, and they had ordered a beautiful cake half decorated for her graduation and half for her birthday. Between laughter and hugs, Celeste enjoys the company of her loved ones, creating unforgettable memories but fun times looks like they run faster! She has to return to resume her activities at her job.

After the party and having remembered happy moments and anecdotes from her childhood, she talks to her mother about her future and tells her that she and Alex plan to live together. He has a couple of jobs in view in the medical area near the university, which would give them all the basics to start a coexistence.

Celeste's mother tells her to follow what her heart feels, but to also think about what she wants her future to be. Celeste is not thinking about marriage, it is not something that crosses her mind.

After spending a short period of enjoyment with her loved ones, and looking forward to her reunion with Alex, she begins her return.

Alex had a key to the apartment and had arrived a couple of days earlier to attend job interviews at a hospital and clinic in the area.

The reunion between Celeste and Alex was very different from what the relationship had been until that moment. They loved each other and the fact that they had left the university behind was like having taken off a shell. They felt freer, different, energized.

A week after, Alex received confirmation that he was offered a contract at the hospital where he had the interview. It was just the missing part so that both could begin to think about what they were going to do with their lives, starting by looking for another place to live. The apartment was good but only for student life.

A couple of months after they had already signed a lease contract for a larger apartment which also had a gym, swimming pool and recreation area.

They both had good taste, they cared about aesthetics, and they liked being in an environment that was welcoming and warm. They were decorating their love nest in their free time, because Alex and Celeste's work sometimes required additional hours beyond normal schedules. Alex because he could be replacing someone who was absent or other eventualities, and Celeste because she had to make up for lost time due to some technical complications and already had the delivery date for her project around the corner.

Thus, the months pass, immersed in their activities, seeking recreation on free days and Celeste continuing with her astrology reading.

At a certain point she tells Alex to do the natal chart to see what comes out. Celeste had read about Synastry, and she needed Alex's natal chart to do it. She was curious to see what would come out in terms of their relationship.

Alex didn't pay much attention to astrology, but since Celeste was interested, he agreed. He had to ask his mother about the time of his birth because he didn't know it.

Alex zodiacal sign is Pisces with an ascendant in Libra. Without a doubt the profession he had chosen merited his astrological characteristics.

From an astrological point of view, the sign and the ascendant say that Alex is a person with empathy and sensitivity: Pisces is a very empathetic and compassionate sign, which combines well with Libra's inclination towards harmony and peace. He has a great ability to understand the emotions of others and to seek conciliation in conflict situations.

Also, can signify a person that can be idealistic and romantic and may even idealize love and relationships.

His creativity and artistic sensitivity are exalted. Above all, represents a person who seeks to get along with others and will always try to avoid conflicts and seek harmony as the axis of his life.

His Sun trine Mars and sextile Pluto explain his inclination for sports, since these planets and aspects put a lot of energy at his disposal.

Alex is surprised when Celeste tells him what appeared in her natal chart because it described aspects of his character in very detail.

Once Celeste has Alex's chart, Celeste does the Synastry comparing both natal charts to see what comes out in terms of the relationship of energies between them.

Their sex life was not only intense but very gratifying. The relationship between Mars and Venus between them precisely marked the energy that they both shared when they made love.

In the synastry they find that Celeste's Pluto squares Alex's Venus. That explains the good sexual relationship they have but also shows that there is an energy that could develop into a problem in the future.

This aspect between these two planets provides emotional intensity and the emotions can become deep and complex, which can lead to situations of great passion and magnetism, but also to intense confrontations.

Pluto, which is on Celeste's chart, may represent the desire for control and taking power in the relationship. It is a aspect to be taken into consideration.

In summary, a square between Venus and Pluto in synastry can indicate significant challenges, but also the opportunity for deep growth and transformation if both are willing to face these challenges and work together to overcome them.

We'll see what happens over time.

TOWARDS THE RETURN OF SATURN

Life passes for both without mayor problems and within a routine. They never discussed having children, it was something not in their mind or priorities, so they used their free time for different activities. The gym, the movies, going out to eat, reading, and other activities keep them occupied.

Alex had gotten a promotion at the hospital and had some schedule changes required by his new role, but that didn't bother Celeste since it was normal for her to work a few extra hours during the week when the job required it.

Celeste's 28th birthday arrives, and she celebrates it with Alex and their friends at a restaurant that Celeste liked which was close to the apartment.

The restaurant was decked out with soft lights and a cozy atmosphere, perfect for a special occasion. Celeste was radiant, celebrating her 28th birthday and she felt a vibrant energy.

The table was decorated with balloons that her friends brought with the number 28.

As they enjoyed a delicious dinner, the conversation turned to astrology, a topic that had captivated Celeste and some of her friends also shared. Between bites of delicious food, they exchanged stories about her zodiac signs, her natal charts, and predictions for the coming year.

Suddenly, someone mentioned the "Saturn return", a significant moment in someone's life that occurs around age 28-30, when Saturn returns to the same position it occupied at the time of birth.

Celeste shared how she had been reflecting on her life and goals during this period, feeling the pressure and drive for growth that Saturn symbolizes.

Alex smiled fondly at her, acknowledging the journey they had taken together during this time of change and discovery. The friends raised their glasses in a toast to Celeste's promising future, full of new experiences and opportunities.

After dinner, it was time for gifts. Celeste opened each one with enthusiasm, thanking each friend for the thought behind each gift. From books on astrology to personalized jewelry, each gift reflected the love and friendship shared at that table.

The highlight came with the birthday cake, lit with flickering candles. Everyone sang "Happy birthday" while Celeste blew out the candles, wishing with all her heart that this year would be as special as the evening she was experiencing.

At the end of the night, Celeste said goodbye to her friends with warm hugs and bright smiles. They left the restaurant, ready to face together everything that the next year, and Celestes's Saturn return had in store for her.

CHANGES AT WORK

A couple of months had passed since her birthday when Celeste arrived at the office and her boss called her into his office. Something had happened, this type of formal meeting was not common when there was fluid and transparent communication between them. Furthermore, Celeste felt a lot of respect and admiration for her boss, since he had not only promoted her from internship to permanent, but the vision and management that he had of the organization and the business were brilliant.

The boss closes the door and begins to explain the situation of the company. Although the company was solid in terms of its financial status and very well positioned in the robotics vertical market, it was privately owned and somehow their growth was limited given extreme competition and keeping up with new technologies.

A global corporation, one of the largest in technology, had been interested in them and despite the fact that there had been secret negotiations for months, now the purchase was about to be finalized.

Celeste remained silent processing that information and no words came out. Thousands of ideas, possibilities, and above all uncertainty passed through her head.

At that moment she remembered what her mother had told her when she graduated, that generally one does not stay working for a lifetime in the same company.

She thought, prediction come true, how right she was!

The first thing that came to mind was that she had to update her resume, which she had never paid attention to, beyond updating her LinkedIn page. She probably needed to start looking for a new job.

Celeste was immersed in all those thoughts when her boss continued with the conversation.

He tells her that he recognizes that this may be a shock for her and apologizes that he could not tell her anything previously because he had signed a 'non-disclosure agreement' when the negotiations began and that prevented him from speaking even with his family about the topic. There was a lot of money at stake because it was a public company.

In any case, he mentioned that her job was not in any danger, beyond the fact that in a 'merger' there are positions that will be eliminated over time. This was not the case with Celeste. Without her knowledge, she had been part of the analysis in the negotiation, and she was proposed to be manager of the foreign offices in the corporation.

The new position required Celeste to travel 50% of the time, at least initially, until she got familiar with offices, employees that she had in charge as well as each office business.

Neither Celeste nor anyone else can be prepared to receive all this information at once and be able to evaluate it accordingly. The mixed emotions that Celeste was going through could be compared to what you feel in any vertigo ride at amusement parks where you move at high speed, and not always with your head up.

Welcome to the corporate life!

From one day to the next, everything can change. Celeste's mother was very clear about it.

Celeste's boss tells her that from that moment on she was part of a small team in charge of the transition of the merger between the two companies, that more than a merger was the integration of the company where she worked with the corporation.

That day was like a before and after in Celeste's life. If her going to college had been a big change for her, what was happening now could not compare.

She had to talk to Alex about it.

Celeste thanks her boss for his considerations and tells him that she supports him in the decisions he makes, but that she needs to organize some of her things. To which the boss responds that it is estimated that it will take about six months to organize the merger, so from now on she will work part-time on the projects she was managing until they were completed, she will not receive new assignments, and for the rest of the time she was devoted to planning for the implementation of the integration, which already had a deadline.

Celeste arrives at the apartment and Alex is already there. It's a weekday but since Alex had to work at the hospital over the weekend he had a couple of days off.

Celeste explained to Alex what happened at work.

They spoke about the possibilities and opportunities they have. Professionally it is a unique opportunity for Celeste, but the issue of travel somewhat complicates their routine.

The return of Saturn in the 10th house of the profession in opposition to its 4th house, and the natal planets that are in her 4th house, clearly explains the energy of the moment.

In the 10th house, Saturn radiates its influence towards the professional field, prompting Celeste to focus all her energy on expanding her career to the maximum. This transit suggests that the decisions and actions she makes now have a significant impact on her future, especially during her next Saturn return between ages 56 and 58.

Astrology, as a guide, indicates the energies of the moment, but it is Celeste who has the final decision-making power. She can choose to accept the new job and immerse herself in the opportunities that arise or choose to accompany the process until the merger is complete and then pursue other career options.

Something important to consider. If Celeste does not take on the responsibilities marked by the energy of the moment, she could be limiting her future possibilities from now until the end of her career, professionally speaking.

For Celeste and any other person with a similar Saturn aspect, if they don't capitalize the possibilities in that period, they will likely have a harder time finding new opportunities until the next Saturn return. This window of time represents a unique opportunity to propel the business career to new heights. If they don't take advantage at this time, a great opportunity will be missed.

Ultimately, Celeste must carefully weigh her options and make a decision that is aligned with her long-term professional and personal goals. If she decides to accept the challenge and work in sync with the energies of the moment, she could open the doors to a bright professional future.

The issue is where Alex fits in all this.

Celeste always prioritized her professional development and perhaps for that reason she was not thinking about marriage or children. She wanted to have someone by her side, to share what a home is, a company that made her feel good and a good sexual relationship. All of that had worked well for her so far. But what would be the future? How might Alex feel about this change?

Many unanswered questions. It was time to start analyzing point by point.

THE CORPORATION

Already during the transition period Celeste was able to verify that the professional life she had led up to that moment, even though she was in charge of a department within the company, was eighty percent technical work and twenty percent managerial. This period of joint work between the consulting company that coordinated the merger, and the participants from the corporation was a completely different world from what she knew.

On the one hand, work hours were indefinite. The goals to be met were well defined and until a step in the process was not completed and approved, they did not move on to the next one. To meet these deadlines the schedule was erratic, it was according to requirements and sometimes been off on weekends was not an option. Not only was the task stressful for Celeste due to the dynamic itself, but she had to deal with people with whom she had no history. She was just learning about the people that she will be working with in her new position in few months.

There were points on which they agreed, but there were others that were more difficult to digest or accept. But as a result, something had become clear to Celeste and that was that the corporation had the final say in everything.

They were very stressful months for Celeste, and little by little she was understanding the scope of everything they were working on and what her participation was in the immediate future.

Although the situation was becoming clearer in regards of work, the situation with Alex was not the same. It was at a very low point. Between Alex's changing schedules due to his work and the lack of predictability of Celeste's schedules, some problems began to arise.

When they were together and wanted to discuss a topic beyond the daily affairs of the home, Celeste was tired and wanted to relax, she didn't want to think about anything. She saw that the control that she used to have over things was difficult now and she was getting stressed out. The situation was leading her, and it seems she had little control over it.

She noticed Alex was distant and found it difficult to find the time or energy to approach him, to get close to him. Her opposition of Saturn with the Moon did not help her. That opposition had activated the natal Moon, Sun, and Mercury conjunction.

She lacked the energy that she had at other times, and she wasn't even going to the gym. It is a period where she saw the glass half empty instead of half full, she saw the negative side of things. The little energy she had was dedicated fully to her work.

She tried to console herself thinking that this is just a period, it will pass, and everything will return to normal...

The merger ended and Celeste was the new director for the global strategic projects of the corporation.

When her mother heard the news, she traveled to visit her. It was a very emotional meeting. While Celeste's mother had been proud of her daughter when she graduated from college, this was no comparison. Her joy filled her in an inexplicable way. She was proud of her daughter, of that little girl who was interested in books when she barely read and asked the why of everything, had become the woman she had in front of her.

It was very important what Celeste had achieved in such a short time.

They spent the weekend together; Alex was working that weekend.

They went to lunch and shopping because Celeste needed a new wardrobe for her new position and her travels. Not that she did not take care of herself before, but now she was representing an important part of the corporation, and she was new. She had to give her best impression ever.

They left no store without a visit, and they returned with so many packages that it was hard for them to fit them all into the car.

Preparation was completed to begin her new path.

She had been assigned an office in a building that the corporation had not far from where the previous company was. Celeste decided to bring some plants and paintings to decorate her new office.

She was assigned a personal assistant who helped her with travel planning, video conferences, and the various administrative activities of her new position. She had to participate in exhibitions and seminars in different places, and in some she had to be the exhibitor of the products or projects that the company was carrying out.

The trips for her first office tour was already organized which would require to be two weeks abroad. There was no point in returning home at the weekend because she would get off the plane and, in a few hours, she would have to leave for the airport again.

She goes with Alex to dinner at the restaurant where she had spent her 28th birthday and they talk about her travel plans. Celeste tells him about the tasks she has to do in the coming weeks.

Celeste tells him that she has to do this until she coordinates and arranges the plans with the foreign offices. After this stage, she could handle things from her office using video conferencing, when possible, instead of traveling.

Alex, according to his natal chart, was a person who avoided confrontation or tried to find a solution without arguing. Born negotiator and willing to always collaborate. But in this case, without making any complaints to Celeste, Alex felt she was distant, very mechanical, very structured. There was nothing he could do to get close to her.

Possibly Celeste was always like that, but at this moment it was like he noticed it more.

They return to the apartment and make love. Celeste was very dominant in the situation, as if she wanted to make a point.

Celeste, being from the sign of Virgo and Alex from Pisces, beyond the rest of the synastry, provide interesting complementary aspects due to the natural differences between them. Virgo tends to be practical, analytical, and focused on details, while Pisces is more intuitive, imaginative, and emotional. This creates an interesting dynamic for them, where Virgo brings stability and order, while Pisces adds emotional depth and creativity.

Since Celeste's Pluto squares Alex's Venus in the synastry, this adds an extra layer of intensity and transformation to the relationship. The square is a tense aspect that can indicate challenges or tensions in the love dynamic. Pluto represents depth, intensity, and transformation, while Venus rules love, harmony, and values.

The intense magnetic attraction that exists between them can also mean emotional conflicts or tensions due to differences in their values or approaches towards love and relationships.

On this night, given the circumstances of what was happening and what was discussed during dinner, Alex felt Celeste's dominant intensity when they made love, and it's like for the first time he feels helpless or even used.

He felt like this was a final release of energy. Something changed or is it something that he just realized.

THE OTHER OFFICES

Celeste sets out on this new adventure and feels prepared for this new test. She only thought about what she could find and tried not to anticipate anything, not to have any preconceptions, just to let herself flow and see where the situation took her.

She had already become familiar with the profile of each office manager, and in general terms what each one worked on. That was a good starting point.

The meetings in the offices went according to plan. Celeste presented what is called the blueprint of the objectives they had, the main roles, responsibilities, and defined the liaison for each office, and returned with the work teams in place.

She was very well received and attended to in each office, they took her to eat at the best restaurants, and even if the time allowed, they took her to visit a particular local place in the area or a tourist attraction.

It was a new sensation for her, receiving so much attention. Although she always was taken into consideration at her previous job, now she was only beginning to realize the importance of the position she was occupying. The attention she received were not personal since they did not know her, they were related to her position in the company.

She decided at that moment to do everything possible to establish a personal relationship and open communication with those responsible for each office, beyond her title. She liked to work within a team at a personal level.

She spoke periodically with Alex, and when she had a moment Celeste sent him photos and comments of the places she was visiting.

Celeste returns home after two intense weeks and resumes work in her office. Her assistant had already prepared the itinerary for the next month.

Upon returning, the situation with Alex seemed more like it was back in college than it was before the merger started. Between working hours and different schedules, the routine between the two was erratic. He was kind, but different.

Celeste may not have realized what was happening at the time, but a potential factor for conflict could be the tension between her ambitious nature and her protective qualities. Balancing her professional aspirations with her commitment to home life is certainly a challenge. There are conflicts and disagreements with Alex about priorities and time management. Alex feels abandoned or overshadowed by Celeste's professional activities creating negative energy in the relationship.

Her Saturn is active at maximum capacity, but it is not only that. Let's remember that astrology is one part, the other part is the life experiences lived in previous years.

For Celeste, having gone through her parents' divorce at a young age, along with her mother's strong will and winning mentality, deeply influences her approach to life, relationships, and personal development.

Having witnessed her mother's resilience and determination firsthand, Celeste likely inherited some of her traits and would embody a similar fighting spirit in her own life. As we saw, Celeste learned from a young age the importance of perseverance, self-sufficiency, and overcoming adversity, while her mother faced the challenges of single parenthood and pursued her own goals and aspirations.

THE SEPARATION WITH ALEX

Months passed when Celeste's routine remained the same, between office and trips, the projects progressed according to plan, and she began to assert herself in her position. Although she was accepted for the position because of the excellent references that her former boss had given her, Celeste's new boss, who was a vice president of the corporation, had been observing her. He had defined her with her peers as extremely intelligent, knowledgeable, diligent, and had excellent skills managing people. Also, that she was polite but direct and effective in her communication. Pluto and Mars in her 3rd house reflects that.

It is not easy to have that type of evaluation in a multinational corporation, most of the time everything happens through politics, which means who you know, is who you are.

Celeste exchanged messages with her previous boss from time to time. She appreciated him very much. He had left by his own decision when the merger was completed. He took home an important amount of money that allowed him his retirement and be free to spend most of his time fishing, which was his hobby and sport, for his enjoyment.

Although on a professional level Celeste's career was on an upward path, her relationship with Alex was on a spiral decline in equal proportion.

As in these types of situations, when someone leaves some place empty, another person or something will eventually fill it in.

Work in a hospital can be very intense and stressful at times. They manage people's lives, and not only with the lives of the patients but also with the family dramas when those treated reach a fatal outcome. It is very rare to see people laughing in a hospital, whether they are those who come to be treated or the employees.

At times doctors and nurses make jokes with patients just seeking to lift their spirits or give them strength to move forward. More than anything, they try to give them good energy.

It is a very exhausting job both from a mental and physical point of view. It is not a job for everyone. Alex handled it well, even though some situations were beyond him.

So, one day he sees the need to support a woman who had lost her mother. Although there was not much that could be done, the situation, the moment, led Alex to console this woman who would be the same age as his or a little older.

Since he was on time for lunch, Alex invites her to have a coffee in the hospital cafeteria to see if he could cheer her up a little. She was waiting for some certificates that they had to give her for her mother's death, and she had to wait an hour for them to be delivered.

In the conversation with this woman, Alex finds out that six months ago she had lost her husband in a traffic accident. They had only been married a couple of years. They didn't have children.

Now she had lost her mother, and she was really feeling bad and alone. She had uncles and cousins who lived in another state, but there was no relative living close to where she lived.

Without knowing this woman's natal chart, without a doubt her 8th house, Pluto and Saturn must have been very active since months ago.

During the conversation something happens between them, the woman felt very comforted by Alex's presence, and he feels very comfortable with her beyond the situation.

After the coffee and an hour-long conversation, Alex must return to work. She thanks him for what he did and gives him her information to keep in touch.

A couple of months passed and one day when Alex was in the apartment alone, because Celeste was away, this woman comes to mind, and he calls her just to check how she was doing.

He finds her much better, recovered, and happy because he had called her. She tells him that she will never forget the support he gave her during such a difficult time. In gratitude and without any obligation, she would like to invite him to eat at an Italian restaurant that she knew, whenever he is available.

Alex hesitates, he doesn't know what to respond, but since it was a kindness for what she had been through, he accepts. They talk on the phone for about half an hour.

That was the beginning of the end of the relationship between Alex and Celeste.

A few months after the dinner that Alex had in the Italian restaurant, he starts a conversation with Celeste explaining how he feels, how things between them do not work anymore, and tells Celeste that he met someone.

He tells her that this woman makes him feel good, makes him feel accompanied and that he wants to spend time with her, and that he is moving out of the apartment.

Celeste does not show any emotion, she listens to him and understands him. Thousands of thoughts passed through her head, and she wondered what they had in common at that moment. And the first answer that came to her mind was, just sharing mutual expenses.

She was dedicated to her work and profession and at that moment, she felt that that was more than enough.

Without drama or problems, they talk about how they do with the apartment and the things they had in common and that was the end of their relationship.

They had a couple of months left on the lease, so Celeste would stay until she finds another place for herself.

THE OPPOSITION OF URANUS

The opposition of Uranus marks a critical point in the life of any individual; it generally occurs between the ages of 40 and 43, since the chronological period depends on the retrograde position of Uranus at the time of birth and the exact moment of the opposition. This period, often compared to the well-known "midlife crisis", marks the beginning of the second half of life.

From an astrological perspective, this period represents a time of transition in which the person no longer considers itself young but does not yet feel completely old. It is a time of deep reflection on the path traveled and evaluation of the achievements and challenges experienced so far.

It should be used to capitalize on the knowledge gained, to make wiser and more meaningful decisions in the future.

On a physical level, it is natural for signs of aging to begin to appear, which can lead to aesthetic concerns and the desire to maintain a more youthful appearance. However, focusing exclusively on physical appearance during this period, would not fully take advantage of the opportunity for personal and spiritual growth that the opposition of Uranus offers.

In the case of our protagonist, whose natal chart shows Uranus in the second house, associated with income, the opposition of Uranus from the eighth house, which deals with shared assets and additional profits, triggers a financial crisis in Celeste's savings.

Celeste and Alex had always kept their finances separate, but shared common financial responsibilities. Celeste, with a higher salary than Alex, had invested a considerable portion of her income in the stock market.

Unfortunately, during the period of Uranus' opposition, a global economic crisis that also affects the country, negatively impacts the value of Celeste's investments. Despite not having bought a house yet, Celeste had plans to do so in the future. The loss in the stock market considerably changes her plans, and contributes to the moment of crisis she experiences at this crucial time in her life.

In short, the opposition of Uranus opens a period of challenge and transformation for Celeste, where she faces deep questions related to her identity, age, and finances.

MEETING A STRANGER

A traditional cafe, situated in the city's suburbs, stands as a cozy and charming retreat for those seeking a respite from the daily grind. Built from what remained of an old house, the business has flourished over time, expanding, and transforming every corner of it into a sanctuary for lovers of coffee and sweets.

Upon entering, the first thing one notices is the wood that dominates the place, which embraces the place with its rustic and homely charm. The aroma of freshly brewed coffee and freshly baked sweets fills the air, enticing the senses to delve into experience and delight.

The carefully selected furniture combines vintage with contemporary, creating a cozy atmosphere. Weathered wood chairs and couches invite you to relax and immerse yourself in the experience, while solid wood tables offer a refuge for lively conversations and quiet moments.

The walls are adorned with decorative art, a mix of paintings by unknown artists and vintage works that add character and personality to the space. The soft lighting, of hanging iron lamps and floor lamps, creates an intimate and cozy atmosphere that invites you to stay a little longer.

In every corner, there are small details that reveal the care and attention to detail that has gone into the design of the place.

Celeste, who had been reading since she was little, was reading at a table far from the entrance door. She liked being there because it gave her an atmosphere different from home and she felt as if she were in a library or bookstore, beyond that the aroma of roasted coffee stimulated her. The place was cozy and for some reason that she still did not understand that place made her feel good, different, in harmony. She felt transported to another place.

She was immersed in reading an astrology book called '*Astrology in the 21st Century*'. What caught her attention the most was that although the book talked about astrology, it related it to the energies, the frequencies, where the planets and their cycles were reflected.

One section talked about prosthetics and artificial intelligence, which caught her attention. It never occurred to her to relate astrology to those topics, but something told her that she had found something that would serve her personal and professional development.

Celeste was immersed in her reading when someone who was sitting at a table next to her spoke to her and asked, 'I saw that you were reading about astrology, what do you think about it?'

Celeste looks up and finds herself in front of a man who would be in his 50s, good looking, elegant with informal but impeccable clothing. His hair, between gray and silver, gives him a distinction that blends harmoniously with his appearance. His features, marked by a firm jaw and expressive eyes, reveal an abundant history of lived experiences.

With a slim build and upright bearing, he conveys a feeling of confidence and kindness. His smile, warm and welcoming, illuminates his face and spreads an aura of friendliness to those around him. The furrows that mark his face tell stories of laughter shared and worries overcome, while his eyes, slightly wrinkled with age, reflect quiet wisdom and innate gentleness.

Celeste was surprised by the question, but after a moment she answered, 'the truth is that it is an exciting and enigmatic topic, mainly because of how old astrology is and for what I am reading, is current in this technological moment that we live in.'

The stranger replies that he is an astrologer, that he has studied astrology for many years and continues to study it, since new things constantly arise for which, it can be applied.

He continues talking about the financial problems that are happening in the world and his vision from the astrological point of view.

Pluto entering the sign of Capricorn was a trigger. The previous time this happened was around 240 years ago. Looking at history and seeing what happened in those days, provide us an idea of what could happen now.

That previous passage of Pluto through Capricorn was the beginning of a process of global structural change, freeing the colonies in America from European reigns. In that period, people began to talk about the 'rights of man', under the slogan 'freedom, equality and fraternity'. A change began that continues to this day in the Western world.

Countries were shaped, new constitutions were drawn up and democracy advanced as a system of government.

At that time, a change began that took time to materialize and that has survived to this day. Most people don't remember or don't recognize what that change signified to people in this part of the world.

This new stage that we are going through will lead us to another profound change in things, as it was the previous time when Pluto entered Capricorn.

Celeste at this moment enters as if into another dimension and is listening with all her senses, trapped by the story. She is in a state of hypnosis.

He continues with his story, Capricorn, which is ruled by the planet Saturn, refers to structures, to organization. We talk about structures of the human body such as the skeletal system, passing through the family structure until we reach governments and world organizations.

Can you imagine what that means? A change that leads us to a new way of life. That change will take a couple of generations to come to fruition, but it has already begun. If you pay attention to the children who are being born and those who will be born during these years, they are the ones who will promote change.

Those who could be left out of touch will be the parents of these children because they are not the ones who are generating change, but their children are.

The parents of these children grew up without the Internet and without cell phones, but they have adopted them as truth and as the only way of functioning and relating to the outside world. Although children take technology as something normal, they will use it to produce a paradigm shift. They are going to be different than their parents who are only technology users.

The financial crisis we are experiencing leads to the fall of these structures because they are simply obsolete. That the stock market is managed by artificial intelligence is giving us an idea that man is leaving the analysis of financial movements to a computer, which can give results in the short term and generate profits, but it is not something that can last over time. The computer can only analyze present trends but cannot understand human thinking and actions.

There is a ceiling for profits and that is set by the cycles. The seven years of the lean cows and the seven years of the fat cows, as mentioned in the Bible and other ancient books, relate to that. These metaphors only indicate that life goes through cycles. No cycle lasts forever. Everything is born, develops and dies.

The dialogue between the two lasted about an hour, with Celeste asking questions and the stranger answering or making comments, always giving examples, or relating the story to something that is known. Mentally, Celeste was analyzing what part of all that affected her in some way.

And just as he appeared, this character kindly said goodbye to Celeste and left the cafe, leaving her a lot of information that would be useful for her future.

She never saw him again.

As it is, it didn't occur to Celeste to ask him if he had social media or any other way to contact him. Celeste was left wondering what had happened, she sensed something but couldn't explain it, but this unexpected interaction had an effect on her and prompted her to delve deeper into the topic.

That meeting had something magical. Who was that man? Where did he come from? Without a doubt he had a purpose for Celeste's life. Things happen for a reason.

THE SECOND HALF OF LIFE

Months pass between projects that were completed, new ones that came to life. It was a routine that had its interesting dynamics.

A period of reflection begins for Celeste, looking back, especially the last few years. For a moment it occurred to her that some concepts that she had handled regarding life were not such. She was rethinking her relationship with Alex, like a movie in fast speed, things were passing through her mind regarding good moments they had lived, the professional development that she had had and maintained, her family, her mother...

It was a moment of confusion. She was wondering, is what I'm doing okay? Is the path I'm on the right one?

She was alone, although she had met a couple of people with whom she had become intimate, like taken some mini-vacation getaways, but nothing that lasted over time.

One of them, whose name was Rodrigo, showed more interest in her, and despite suggesting meeting more frequently, she kept her distance from him.

Rodrigo had his import and export business, he was in a very good financial position like Celeste, and he was divorced. Rodrigo traveled constantly due to his work, which also allowed Celeste the freedom that she did not have to respond to invitations for dinners every weekend.

They usually met once or twice a month when they both happened to be in town and not traveling.

Celeste continued traveling to the offices and although not as often as she initially did, because she was able to consolidate a work group that produced excellent results.

Celeste had been promoted to Senior Director and she achieved a position and a good reputation within the company. Some predicted for her the vice presidency of the division she managed or something more than that.

She had developed her potential to the maximum, but there is always a but, she had not worked on her limitations. These were well marked in her natal chart.

Celeste had delved deeper into the topic of astrology; she had done an online workshop that had provided her with a lot of information for additional research and development.

Although she had not taken a formal astrology course, with the amount that she read, researched and so on, she was an expert on the subject.

At this time in life, she thought she had to stop and analyze in depth how she had gotten to where she was and what options were available for her future.

She decided to take a few days of vacation. Usually, she had only gone out on long weekends with some additional days when she went on a getaway with Rodrigo. Their preferred place was the islands in the Caribbean.

Celeste asked her assistant to find her a resort hotel on the Pacific Ocean in Mexico. She wanted to go on vacation for a week. Somewhere quiet and that gave her the possibility of leisure activities.

Of the options presented by her assistant, Celeste thought the Ixtapa proposal was the best. She had never been to that place which offered her the possibility of something new while she rested.

Celeste's purpose was to go to a place that can provide entertainment and relaxation that will allow her to process all the astrological information she had about her and see if that helped her organize at least her immediate future. There were things that she knew she had done well and others that she was not so convinced.

She arrived at the resort in Ixtapa, and the beauty of the place was superior to the videos and photos she had seen. That place had a different, energizing energy.

Upon entering the spacious lobby, she already appreciates the excellence of the place. Large windows where natural light enters, with spaces designed with exquisite attention to detail. Warm tones and fine wood touches are combined with contemporary design elements. A central fountain produces the soft sound of running water and is adorned with tropical flowers. The furniture distributed asymmetrically throughout the lobby is comfortable and luxurious.

There are luxury boutiques offering local artisanal products, as well as elegant lounges that make up the main restaurant and bar with a stunning view of the Pacific Ocean.

Celeste smiles and thinks, just what I need!

She does the checking, and they accompany her to the suite she had reserved. The stewardess shows her all the amenities at her disposal and leaves her wishing her an excellent stay.

Celeste opens the balcony door of the suite that has an incredible ocean view where a panorama of great beauty unfolds. In front, the vast Pacific Ocean stretches as far as the eye can see, with its blue and turquoise waters merging with the horizon in a spectacle of serenity and beauty.

She can see sailboats and yachts near the port to her left, the expanse of white sand beach, fringed by palm trees and the brightly colored umbrellas that look like decoration from a distance. The island in front of the resort is the only thing that interrupts the horizon line of the sea.

At that moment she felt a sensation of pleasure, of harmony, of peace that she had not experienced in a long time. She understood that she was doing what she had to do, it was the right time and in the right place. The stars accompanied her.

A good transit of Jupiter with her natal Jupiter and Venus generated that energy. It could even happen that she meets someone or that her love life takes a good turn...

The energy of the planetary aspects active in question indicate this possibility.

But Celeste had in mind to do a thorough analysis of her natal chart, the transits, her life and see if she could draw some conclusion about the changes she should make. Something had to change, and she was looking for information that would help her make the change.

A phrase came to her mind that some credit to Albert Einstein that says, 'dementia is always doing the same thing and expecting a different result.' Regardless of the origin of said phrase, it was true. Something told Celeste that some things had to be changed, the point was to discover what they were.

The positive things in Celeste's life were very well marked in her natal chart and her life path up to this point clearly demonstrated that she had acted in them and was now enjoying the results.

Of the negative things, if we can call them that, the issue of losing money in the stock market was very clear to her because she thought she could have prevented it in some capacity if she knew what was coming. Leason learned the hard way, now she already knew how to deal with it in the future.

But there was something else that occupied her mind. While she was dealing with the issues of her work, which demanded a good part of her daily time since the offices she was managing were in different time zones, she functioned fully. But when there was silence, peace, something was missing. She felt like a void.

On her laptop she had an astrology program, and, on her phone, she had installed an app from a well-known astrologer named Jimena. This app managed the natal chart data and made projections about upcoming transits and gave suggestions on how to carry them forward according to the impact they had. The user had to answer certain questions to the program and depending on the answers, with all the data available, it will indicate the weak points, the strong points and those to be defined. Over time, the program will tell her which things she had to improve that she had not done, for example, or things that were good previously but decreased in level. The purpose was for the person to be able to periodically monitor its evolution process.

In personal things as in life, it is useless to be excellent in one subject and poor in another. You must always seek balance, which is not easy.

Celeste finds that between her natal chart, transits and answers to the questionnaire, her deficiency was related to her fourth house, the home.

The home is not only the house, the furniture, or the comfort that one may have, the home is the set of energies that exist produced by the physical and human components that are generated by coexistence. Each of the parts generates its own energy, which adds or conditions each other.

Celeste's natal Saturn is an energy activator on a social level that, when used correctly, guarantees success in the profession and a good social status. This position shows others that you are someone with a solidity and structure that allows the person to assume great responsibilities. The person has all the natural tools to take them on.

The problem with a Saturn in the tenth house when this takes precedence over the rest of things, is that it can result in a lack of attention to the home, which is represented by the opposite house in the natal chart, the fourth house.

In the case of Celeste, in the fourth house she has the Moon, the Sun and Mercury. She needs home life, she needs family, that aspect is also native to her. Because of the choices and decisions Celeste made previously, this is an aspect that she has left aside.

With Alex, the possibility of starting a family was never present. They felt good and that relationship could have worked for any other couple, but not for the two of them.

Alex's family was never integrated with Celeste's family, or Celeste's to Alex's. This may not be necessary or conditional for anyone else, but for Celeste it was, because her DNA required it. Without realizing it, she focused on the profession only and left that aspect aside.

There was neither time nor conditions to have children, either now or in the future. Without descendants, what family could she have left when Celeste's grandparents and parents were no longer around? However, her DNA, her natal chart, required that.

It is good for those not familiar with astrology what information you can find in a natal chart. Beyond the zodiac sign which determines that a person is of any given sign, this is only one characteristic within a larger puzzle that must be analyzed as a whole.

If those natal characteristics summarized in capabilities and restrictions were known at certain development time in life, it would be easier for the person to see where they should focus their attention. Natal restrictions are of utmost importance since these will have their weight on the individual's adult life. The midlife crisis brings them to light.

If one focuses one's life only on one's professional career or business, or only family for example and leaves aside the rest of the areas that make a person whole, at some point in life a crisis will occur.

Crises must be seen as opportunities for changing things; if there is a crisis, one must analyze how one got into that situation. Don't blame others but check what decisions you made to get to that point.

Celeste begins to understand her situation. She understands that in life there are moments for everything. She is in her mid-forties, so she can't even think about children. But with respect to the home, what can be done? She feels that she needs it, she is missing something, she is not complete without it.

As they say, everything can be fixed as long as there is life. The issue is finding how to fix it.

Celeste was aware of the conversation she had had with the astrologer in the cafe. The change coming globally impacted everyone and could even have an effect on her work. Companies related to technology, which was her market, had been the least affected by the financial problem, but no one could guarantee that in the future that would be different. She had to think about herself, about her future.

Over the years she had not worried about having his own house because she did not want to have to think about its maintenance and other things that a house entails, but now it was different. She was determined to buy a house, all she had to do was decide where and when.

By using astrology, which she had used mainly to aid her in his profession, it could also provide her with information about the best period to look for and buy a home. Usually just avoiding complicated planetary transits is enough.

She also knew about certain places and the different energy that a place could have. The house was not going to be where she lived now, she was thinking more long term. Would it be near the sea or in the mountains? She hadn't defined it yet, but it wouldn't be in a big city.

The mere fact of having made that determination made her feel good. She felt like she had opened a door that was closed and with that she saw a new path opening ahead of her. It was a purpose unlike any other she had before.

Between walks on the beach, bathing in the sea, snorkeling excursions, and the spa, four comforting days went by.

She talks to Rodrigo and tells him where she is, and about her ideas and the plans she is giving shape to. He answers that he is traveling to be with her until she returns.

Rodrigo arrives at the resort, which is also new to him. He also feels a different energy in that place, he feels good.

Goes to Celeste's room and she receives him with a long and warm kiss. Immediately he felt that something had changed between them from the last time they were together. There was something he could not explain, it was another energy between them. It felt really good.

Rodrigo sees Celeste more relaxed, more open, as if she had taken off a shell that was containing her.

Beyond that, she was radiant, tanned, sensual. She looked like another woman. They make love and even that was different. It was less mechanical, more caressing, more energized but relaxed, they had to make that moment last forever. They fall asleep hugging each other like it has never happened before.

They spent a few days that can be defined as perfect. From the place, the weather, how they felt.

In their long talks, when they were not on the beach or making love, Celeste tells him what she was thinking and the idea she has. Rodrigo had wanted to spend more time with her for a long time, but her career and business always took priority.

Celeste tells him what she needs, she tells him that she is missing that home that she once had and that it was gone.

Rodrigo lived alone like Celeste; by their age it was time to start thinking about how to spend the future they had. Rodrigo was 9 years older than Celeste, so he also thought about having someone with whom he could share the rest of his life.

Although Rodrigo was not interested in astrology, Celeste had asked him for his birthday information to see her synastry with him. She finds that there were positive aspects of Mars and Venus between the two, a good aspect between Rodrigo's Saturn and Celeste's Venus, so from an astrological point of view, that marked either the age difference between them or that Rodrigo was somehow the more mature of them. There were no major negatives aspects between the slow planets and the rest between them. That guaranteed a certain stability in the couple, beyond the fact that each one could go through complicated transits at some point, but it would not be given to both of them at the same time.

Celeste tells him that she wants to buy a house to eventually live in, either when she retires or before, but that she felt it was necessary. She needed a place to say that's my house, that's my home.

Because of his business, Rodrigo had contacts in different parts of the world, and given the current conditions on a global scale in general, he told her that it would be good to define the place where to buy first and then look for a home. She even considered buying something that would be used on vacation first and at some point, move in permanent.

CELESTE AND RODRIGO

Back to the routine of the company and business, both had the need to see each other more frequently. The talks continued regarding the best places to buy a property, each one giving a vision of things according to the information they had.

After a couple of months of the trip to Ixtapa, they decide to go and live together in Rodrigo's apartment.

From the outcome, it seems that Celeste's Jupiter transit really paid off. If this relationship began under those astrological aspects, they were undoubtedly auspicious, for both beyond Rodrigo's transits.

Sometimes things can start well, but when the natal charts and the synastry is analyzed in detail, there could be one or several aspects that were not seen, but that come to light over time.

Celeste gives a feminine touch to Rodrigo's apartment, which he likes very much. From the decoration to the furniture that she changed; it gives a different life to the same apartment. From something cold and businesslike, it becomes something warmer and more welcoming.

Thus begins this new path in the life of our protagonist.

From the evolutionary point of view, we see what results can be achieved simply by working on the complicated points of the natal aspects. First of all, we must recognize them, there is no point in trying to solve a problem if we do not have a good definition of it. It is very common to see people blaming someone else for all their problems, but on the other hand they never really looked in the mirror to see how they are, or why they do what they do.

Celeste took the opportunity that her Uranus opposition gave her to see herself, to learn from herself, to understand why she made the decisions that she made, and the rest of the things that compose the path of a human life on earth. It is very important not to make judgment, it is a moment of analysis, to get into the essence of things, see what worked well and what needs to be improved.

This process must be done without blaming oneself, without looking for culprits to discharge one's own ineptitude, and above all things, understand where our ideas or acts come from.

THE END OF LIFE

Everything is in the past for Celeste. Her parents, her grandparents, her uncles had already left the game. She and Rodrigo continue their life together. They were both in good health, had a very good financial situation, and both enjoyed each other's company. They had both worked very hard throughout their lives, and for different reasons had given up their family lives. Now was their chance to get some of that back. It's never too late.

Celeste sometimes thought, what if she had met him before, and if we had had children, and so many other questions that we human beings ask about the past.

The reality is that we were making decisions as opportunities presented themselves and it is most likely that the decision that was made ten years ago could now be different, but what is not always understood is that it took ten years of experience to being able to think differently.

It is clear that life is a learning experience but living it in every sense of the word is not just passing through it. It's making decisions, learning from mistakes and improving, there is always room to learn something. That learning is the purpose we have here on this plane, it is our 'contract' that we define ourselves before coming. We choose the beginning and from the moment we are conscious we become totally responsible for our lives, our destiny.

Above all things, the BEING is responsible for itself, and this responsibility cannot be delegated.

A person can be helped, someone can ask for support, and be provided, but under no circumstances can anyone take charge of another life. That would interfere with free will, which is the most precious thing one has.

Celeste recognized her failure and looked for a way to solve it. We all have our Saturn. It is the backpack with which we are born, and it is during our lifetime, by using our consciousness as a guide, that we learn to manage it. To ignore it and look the other way and say that we have overcome it, that would be a double mistake. Thinking that we have overcome something when in reality we hide it and convince ourselves that it does not exist has consequences.

We will be our own judge and determine whether we achieve our goals or not. No one will judge us or defend us; everything begins and ends with oneself. But that is in the next stage, on the one we are still in, it would be a mistake to think that the laws of the universe can be deceived. Here and anywhere else, actions have consequences.

THE RETURN HOME

After the time it takes to disconnect Celeste's consciousness from the earthly plane, which is a process that takes a few days, the same journey begins in reverse from when she reached her mother. The same acceleration, the same vision of the planets, the galaxies and instead of finding darkness as when she arrived at her mother, she sees an immense light that blinds her.

Times are measured differently depending on where one is in the universe, and what was a life on Earth could have been one day where Celeste comes from.

She finds herself at the place from where her journey began. She is lying comfortably in the couch bed.

If we want to see it from a physical point of view, Celeste never left that couch or that place, her consciousness was the one that left her to connect to earth.

When on earth its mention about connecting with the 'Higher Self' they are simply saying, connecting with our very essence, which is where we come from.

The Akashic records connect with the source where all the information is stored. We all have the possibility of accessing it, but from the earth' plane it is not easy with all the conditioning and preconceptions that exist. We are in a dense plane of low vibration.

Let's continue calling our character Celeste, even though she is no longer Celeste, but rather she returns to her essence which has countless experiences sometimes with a name, other times not, which occurred previously in different galaxies, planets, and times.

Someone whose job is at the center where Celeste is, approaches her and brings her a glass of energized water and smiles at her. These experiences are not easy to go through, beyond the fact that they are done at will and are important for the development and expansion of consciousness.

Let's make the parallel when one goes to college. The person takes a new class, it knows that the teacher is demanding, the subject to be studied is complicated, its classmates are new, so it is a new experience. From the homework to be done, studying, the new topic to learn and exams, all of this generates some stress.

We could say that something similar happens with an experience on earth. Beyond learning, the essence that embodies is previously present in an environment where everything is order, harmony, and peace. This is because it is at a level that requires certain advances in the evolutionary process to belong to. Going to earth, to deal with earthly issues has its load of stress.

The being who attends Celeste exchanges telepathic thoughts with Celeste while she takes sips of the water. Celeste has all the information about her life and somehow tries to organize it chronologically to have a sequence. Her consciousness is integrating the experience of the earth with all of her previous existence.

After a while she feels good, she is back to the status she was in before this last experience. Celeste is in a large room, where a considerable number of similar devices are located. All of those beings present were experiencing a similar experience to what Celeste had and not necessarily all on earth. They could have gone to any of the existing worlds in the galaxy they are in or in other galaxies.

When we were talking about the AI selecting the parents and the correct moment to come down to earth, to determine that, the amount of information that had to be processed is unimaginable.

Let's think about the earth 30 years ago, who would have imagined the internet, Google, and Artificial intelligence. Now let's just try to imagine the amount of information that must be handled at the planetary level, including solar systems, and galaxies. Everything is connected, everything is part of the whole. The universal internet managed by AI.

Celeste leaves the soul connection center and returns to her 'home'. She shares the place where she lives with others who are at the same level of consciousness as her. Her existence is similar to the earth, but very different in several aspects.

At that level of consciousness, feelings or states of mind do not exist as they are experienced on earth. There is only the reflection of what a feeling could be. Celeste remembers each event that she experienced on earth, but not the feeling that each event had, such as joy, sadness, or indifference.

Food is limited to something that could be defined as energetic water, which is what is required for subsistence and not as a pleasure as happens on earth.

The relationships between beings are given by energetic exchange, which is what we could define as love. But not physical love but spiritual. There are no different sexes or sexual activity. A being in a certain evolutionary state can unfold and 'create' one or more beings of the same essence. That is another process for which there is an area in charge of carrying this out when the conditions are given.

Everything is very detailed diagrammed and works without errors. Everything has a reason and above all things, a purpose.

Celeste communicates with her housemates, and they exchange information about the different things that each one has done during the day. They have different responsibilities, tasks to perform and objectives. Everyone contributes to a common good with the purpose of raising awareness.

The different evolutionary levels are very varied, and some are difficult to understand on an earthly level.

Celeste shares with her clan her experiences, her learning, the mistakes she made, what goals she achieved and what she did not, making a balance far above what she experienced on earth.

The experience provides a grade or qualifying note as a result, and depending on this, the next experience will be based on previous results.

When we talked about how the AI evaluates the information entered by Celeste for her descent to earth, it also considers all of her background and only then assigns the place and conditions for her arrival.

The conditions of the next experiences will be based on the levels acquired in the sum of the previous ones. That is why the evolution of a soul takes millions of incarnations to perfect itself and raise consciousness.

Only the area of connection with the earth and the area of multiplication of beings was mentioned, but there are a large number of corporeal or ethereal organisms at a universal level with different responsibilities and tasks. Every requirement has to be attended to; nothing is left to chance.

An organization that should interest us as human beings above all things is the 'Council of Love'. The Council is in charge of seeing the evolutionary degrees of each planet, and seeing how they advance according to the general plan. According to the progress, the possible actions to be taken will be determined considering the objectives of the evolutionary process.

The Council decides whether help should be sent to raise the consciousness of the planet if the analysis carried out shows that it is not evolving according to the plan. Each plan has its variations and certain deviations are allowed. If it is seen that the planet is stagnant in its evolutionary process or in decline, the possibilities of help are analyzed.

To talk about the earth, which is what is best known, beings like Buddha, Jesus, Krishna, Muhammad, and many other beings whose names are not known have passed by. They were sent to awaken human consciousness because evolution was stagnant on a planetary level.

If we see the known history on earth, the arrival of help does not guarantee good results. Wars, human abuse, materialism above all things and the poor treatment of nature, among others, the objectives of the help sent were not achieved. The messengers who preached love and empathy between human beings have been misinterpreted or ignored over time.

In the same way, when several rescue attempts have failed, after intense analysis the council has the power to decide on an end to the cycle and it must begin a new cycle. That happens when the result of the analysis is that it can no longer be fixed.

Starting over means a reset and the most common way to do this is through a global catastrophe. One could take what is known as the universal flood as one of those events.

On earth there are countless vestiges of ancient civilizations that had an Incredibles development and also disappeared, leaving only the ruins as a witness that at some point they populated the earth.

Like the Council of Love, there are also councils that are in charge of the evolution process of plants and animals since they also have degrees of consciousness of different levels. Universal structures have their complexity and are necessary to carry out the total evolutionary process.

In essence, the universe works with laws, which are universal and no one and nothing escapes them. On earth, man defines laws that may or may not be aligned with universal laws. If the earth's laws defined by human beings are not aligned with the universal laws, these may be one of the reasons why civilizations do not advance, stagnate, and disappear.

In the same way that in any country no law can go against the founding constitution, earth's laws cannot go against universal laws, but it is common for human beings to do so. This is one of the causes where evolution stagnates or regresses. Mainly for not respecting universal laws.

One example known is the law of not to kill. Man cannot have a law that destroys what has been created, which is superior to man himself. Nothing can justify the death of another, not even war. This denotes the lack of existing awareness.

The other case is that earthly laws may be well-intentioned in their enunciation but poorly applied in their concept. For example, the fact that children have to be educated is a well-intentioned obligation, but that they are educated according to the political color of a certain moment means that the personal development and conscience of the child are not taken into consideration. The development of consciousness is the first purpose of existence.

This is a universal law.

In certain cases, universal laws will apply whether or not they are accepted by humans. And when things are far from what they are expected, things happen to what's known since ancient times as *Ordo ab Chao*, Order to Chaos.

LEVELS OF EXISTENCE

There are levels of existence in the universe and what concerns us as human beings because it is within our sphere of consciousness, are the levels within reach of where we are.

They are the twenty-one levels of existence at the physical level on earth. These are within the first 49 levels of existence, which could have 'communication' with the earth. The levels above 49 are on another higher evolutionary plane of existence and have no relationship with the lower levels.

All level groups are related to the number seven.

The first three levels are physical; They include plants, animals, and humans.

The first level

This level has a lower vibrational frequency, which is blue in color. Allows the consciousness of the self to make a smooth transition. This level is the basis of the other levels within that plane of existence.

The second level

It is the highest vibrational level and is red in color. This is a mirror level of the first level.

They are the opposite and complement the first level. When a being is at this level, he develops an awareness of the entire reality of the plane in which he finds himself.

It is an awareness of all the senses, it is a reality in which it is total immersion, which is given by the 5 senses. This plane is for learning.

The third level

This level has a different intensity, more aimed at the development of inner consciousness, and the color is yellow. This level goes through the other two previous levels.

At this level you can reach other life forms on the same plane more directly.

Like the two previous levels, it is horizontal and cannot ascend or descend. It's for learning.

The fourth level

The color of this level is pink. It is the level where you can contact other entities at other levels. This plane is the beginning of the ascension or descent, it creates unity with all the other planes.

The main quality of this plane is what we call LOVE (not as is known on earth level).

Achieves openness to other realities outside of the material.

The fifth level

The color of this level is green. This is a healing light and works very closely with the fourth level. The two levels are interrelated.

This level is presented by great inner peace, it gives great tranquility due to the development of consciousness, it is the consciousness of love. This is a descending level, where the being is more aware of the reality of the previous levels. This level provides an understanding of reality.

The sixth level

The color of this plane is purple (a different type of purple) This is an ascending level and creates an awareness of the possibility of reaching the next levels. In this reality, the being can transcend the plane where he is located.

The fifth and sixth levels are very interesting and there are very few beings that exist at these levels.

The seventh level

The color for this level is white. This level closes the first evolutionary circle, and the being has complete consciousness and understanding of reality. Consciousness is not only for the level of the self, but also for all levels that could be in contact.

This level is vertical and touches all other levels of existence. This level is the one that harmonizes and unites all the other levels. This is the highest plane of reality in which one can exist in physical form.

Animals exist from the eighth to the fourteenth plane.

When a consciousness reaches the fourteenth level, it can no longer go higher unless it is willing to change its form of consciousness.

Levels fifteen to twenty-one are what is called human life on earth.

When a person reaches level twenty-one, they have the option to go higher or remain in human form. To go higher he has to give up incarnating in human form.

Levels twenty-two to twenty-eight are a bridge. These are the levels that the human being enters when he dies and returns to the origin from which he comes.

When a consciousness reaches level twenty-eight, a bridge is crossed, and to continue its evolution, it cannot take human form of any kind. It can do it like any other form of life but not as a human.

When a soul reaches a level of consciousness higher than forty-nine, it can no longer have communication with the lower levels of consciousness.

These different levels provide just a glimpse of the complexity of the functioning of the universe and also details the coexistence on earth of different degrees of consciousness at the same time. This makes existence very complex and with a lot of possibility of trying different experiences.

Other planets that are more advanced from an evolutionary point of view are more harmonious and homogeneous in terms of their structure and coexistence, making any experience more predictable.

If we see on earth the different cultures, races, countries, religions, political views and other things that separate and divide people, added to this, we are at a dense level of low vibration and motivated by emotions, experiences. They become more than interesting.

From a religious point of view, the levels previously defined are also mentioned by different religions. For example, the Catholic Church recognizes the different celestial hierarchies as follows.

First hierarchy

Seraphim

Cherubs

Thrones
Second hierarchy
Dominations
Virtues
Powers
Third hierarchy
Principalities
Archangels
Angels

Each one represents an evolutionary level which gives them different capacities and functions, and they are in charge of certain celestial tasks or communication with humans.

The other religions divide the celestial hierarchical levels in a different way, but they recognize the existence of different degrees of consciousness in the universe.

Celeste, due to her evolutionary degree and experience, has a group of people on Earth assigned to her to provide guidance, we can say that's her 'job'. Her task is to connect with them, without interfering in their actions and allowing the exercise of their free will, to help them in their evolutionary process.

Just like what happened to her in her last experience and everybody else, it is not easy to arrive and start something new with no memory of what came before.

On the earth's level, this new being will depend, since an infant on the love it receives, education and shelter as a fundamental basis. The conditioning of the family tree is a factor that cannot be ignored, added to subsequent education and the experiences that one goes through.

It is said that human beings can start evolving their consciousness after the age of 40-43, identified by astrology by the opposition of Uranus. This could be a critical time of development, as it is a time of balance in life. The path traveled is observed and that is when conclusions are drawn.

The second part of life that is a new beginning and offers the possibility of developing everything from previously learned experiences. This is an opportunity, but its development is not guaranteed; it will depend on each person how they use their free will.

Celeste, in her task, 'connects' with the people she has in charge of, seeing how their lives go, and she will try to provide the help they need. It will be presented to them in the form of dreams, books, movies, videos, people, and anything that gives them a clue to a solution or information for the situation they are going through.

It is not guaranteed that the person will recognize these messages. Celeste will not be graded on the person's success or failure, but on the support, she gave them. The result does not depend on her.

Any of us can see how many things in our daily lives were done or avoided because a 'message' somehow arrived and that made us change our decision.

The 'astrologer' that was introduced to Celeste at the cafe could well have been one of those interventions that human beings receive, which have a purpose. Whether we realize it or not, whether we pay attention to it or not, will depend on each one of us. But help is always available.

We just have to thank that superior being who is guiding us, who is seeking the best for each one. We have to be open to receive that communication, which has no type of limitation, as long as it is to improve and evolve.

Celeste's life thus passes through her routine while she does work to raise consciousness and thinks about her next experience on earth which will occur after the great changes that she knows are coming.

Probably in her next experience she may return as someone who manages and aligns the energies at a personal level on Earth, in order to help those who survived the end of the current cycle.

ENZO

In the city of Buenos Aires, Argentina, in the first days of August, a male baby is born.

The nurse looks at the clock on the wall of the nursery which reads 11:45 am.

It was a rainy and cold day but for Enzo's parents that did not matter, the moment they had been waiting for had arrived, their son had been born...

To be continue...

Check our blog @ www.elnuevocamino.com
The Game of Life

About the Author

Edu Petriati, a computer scientist and astrologer, introduced a new look at astrology in 2018 with the book Astrology in the 21st Century, which was followed by Astrology in the 21st Century – Evolution. His extensive career in the technological sector and after years of studying and practicing astrology, he presents this book as a proposal seeking to delve into the reason for life, before and after passing through this plane and seeing the purpose behind the things.

Read more at https://www.elnuevocamino.com.